— Discovering Canada —

# George Vancouver

Weigl
CALGARY
www.weigl.ca

Erinn Banting

Published by Weigl Educational Publishers Limited
6325 – 10 Street SE
Calgary, Alberta, Canada
T2H 2Z9

Web site: www.weigl.ca

**Library and Archives Canada Cataloguing in Publication**
Banting, Erinn, 1976-
        George Vancouver / Erinn Banting.
(Discovering Canada)
Includes index.
ISBN 1-55388-067-6 (bound).--ISBN 1-55388-120-6 (pbk.)
        1. Vancouver, George, 1757-1798--Juvenile literature.
2. Northwest Coast of North America--Discovery and exploration--
British--Juvenile literature.  3. Pacific Coast (B.C.)--Discovery and
exploration--British--Juvenile literature.  4. Explorers--Great Britain--
Biography--Juvenile literature.  5. Explorers--Canada--Biography--
Juvenile literature.  I. Title.  II. Series: Discovering Canada (Calgary, Alta.)

G246.V3B35 2005          j971.1'01'092          C2005-900496-7

Printed in the United States of America
1 2 3 4 5 6 7 8 9 0    09 08 07 06 05

We acknowledge the
financial support of the
Government of Canada
through the Book
Publishing Industry
Development Program
(BPIDP) for our
publishing activities.

**PROJECT COORDINATOR**
Janice L. Redlin

**COPY EDITOR**
Tina Schwartzenberger

**DESIGN**
Terry Paulhus

**LAYOUT**
Kathryn Livingstone

**PHOTO RESEARCHERS**
Jennifer Hurtig
Heather Kissock
Kathryn Livingstone

**On the Cover**
George Vancouver is
remembered as a very
thorough explorer of
the western coast of
North America.

# CONTENTS

# Introduction

George Vancouver led the longest mapping expedition in history. His 4.5-year journey began in 1791. Throughout their years of travel, Vancouver and his crew sailed about 140,000 kilometres. They journeyed along North America's coast from northern Mexico to southern Alaska. Much of the coast had not been **surveyed**. Many of his measurements were so accurate that they are still used today.

- George Vancouver's career had three distinct stages. His early years were spent voyaging with James Cook. His middle years were spent on ships in the Caribbean. Vancouver's later career years were spent discovering North America's west coast.

## Explorer Essentials

Vancouver was a skilled mapmaker and **navigator**. He took many measurements of the land he explored.

**Curiosity about wealth and need for simplified trade routes drove European explorers to sail across the ocean.**

**985** The Vikings first visited Canada's northeastern regions.

**1000** Viking Leif "the Lucky" Ericson reached Canada. He settled in Vinland, which may be the area now known as L'Anse aux Meadows in Newfoundland and Labrador. Archaeologists found Viking artifacts in this area in the 1960s.

By the 1800s, traders from Russia and Europe had settled in Alaska and on the west coast of what is now Canada. They wanted to work in the fur trade. The traders believed they could earn a large amount of money in Canada. The fur trade was a very successful industry at this time.

- A steering wheel is connected to a rudder located at the rear end of a boat. The rudder is a flat piece of wood or metal that can be turned side to side in the water, controlling the direction a boat travels.

**1576** Martin Frobisher journeyed to what is now Canada to search for the **Northwest Passage**. Frobisher and his crew became the first Europeans to sail into Hudson Strait.

**1668** Pierre-Esprit Radisson and Médard Chouart, Sieur des Groseilliers, sailed to what is now Canada to join the fur trade. They entered Hudson Bay and established the area's first trading post.

**1790s** George Vancouver searched for the Northwest Passage. He sailed about 15,000 kilometres along North America's Pacific coast.

**1808** Simon Fraser wanted to discover a route from the Rocky Mountains to the Pacific Ocean. He explored a river now named after him. Fraser followed the Fraser River to the Pacific Ocean.

# Early Years

**V**ancouver was born in 1757 in King's Lynn, one of Great Britain's busiest **ports**. He had always wanted to explore the exciting seas and lands beyond his home country. Vancouver joined the Royal Navy at 13 years of age. The Royal Navy defended Great Britain from attack by sea.

■ Vancouver's birthplace, King's Lynn, has played a role as an import centre since the twelfth century.

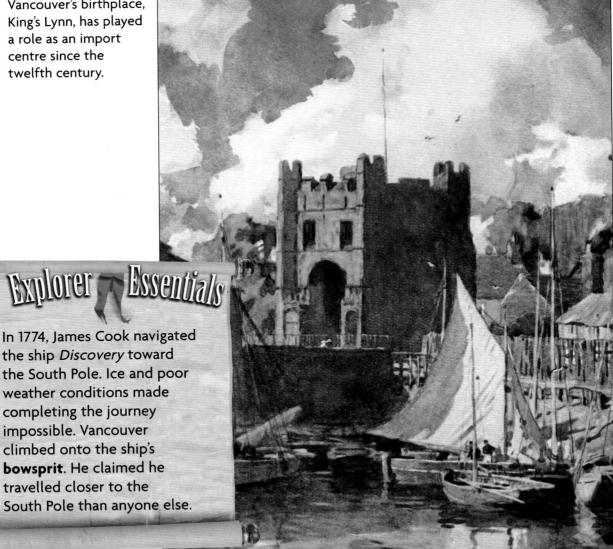

## Explorer Essentials

In 1774, James Cook navigated the ship *Discovery* toward the South Pole. Ice and poor weather conditions made completing the journey impossible. Vancouver climbed onto the ship's **bowsprit**. He claimed he travelled closer to the South Pole than anyone else.

In 1772, Vancouver joined the crew on a ship captained by James Cook. At the time, Cook was one of the most successful and admired explorers in Great Britain. Cook explored the Pacific Ocean and west coast of North America. Vancouver was part of Cook's crew on two of Cook's most important voyages. Between 1772 and 1775, Vancouver joined an expedition to the newly discovered **continent** of Australia. Between 1776 and 1780, he helped explore the Hawai'ian Islands, the west coast of what is now Canada, and Alaska. Vancouver became a skilled navigator and mapmaker on these voyages.

■ James Cook was the first person to cross the Antarctic Circle. He did this in 1773.

## The Northwest Passage

European explorers began searching for the Northwest Passage in the 1400s. They sailed the waters of the Atlantic Ocean to the Canadian Arctic. John Cabot, Jacques Cartier, Martin Frobisher, John Davis, and Henry Hudson searched for the mysterious passage. Some people thought there might be a way to cross the North American continent by ship. Such a passage would make it easier for Europe to trade with Asia by providing a shorter route. The explorers did not find the Northwest Passage. Instead, exploration to the interior of Canada was opened up. In the 1700s, other Europeans decided to begin searching for a passage through Canada from the Pacific Ocean to the Atlantic Ocean. By the end of Vancouver's expedition, he discovered that such a passage did not exist south of Alaska.

# Vancouver's Ventures

**S**oon after returning to Great Britain, Vancouver was made a **lieutenant** in Great Britain's Royal Navy. For the next 9 years, he served on warships in the Caribbean Sea. The ships had been sent to protect British land and citizens. The ships carried goods to and from the Caribbean Islands.

In 1790, the Royal Navy made Vancouver captain of his own ship. He was hired to lead an expedition to map the west coast of North America. As well, the Royal Navy wanted Vancouver to search for the Northwest Passage. He was also asked to reclaim land contested by the Spanish in Nootka Sound.

- Between 1780 and 1789, Vancouver served on three warships in the Caribbean. They were named *Martin*, *Fame*, and *Europa*.

## Explorer Essentials

When Vancouver first visited the west coast of Canada, he believed Nootka Sound was part of an island. It is part of Vancouver Island. To honour George Vancouver, Vancouver Island was named after him.

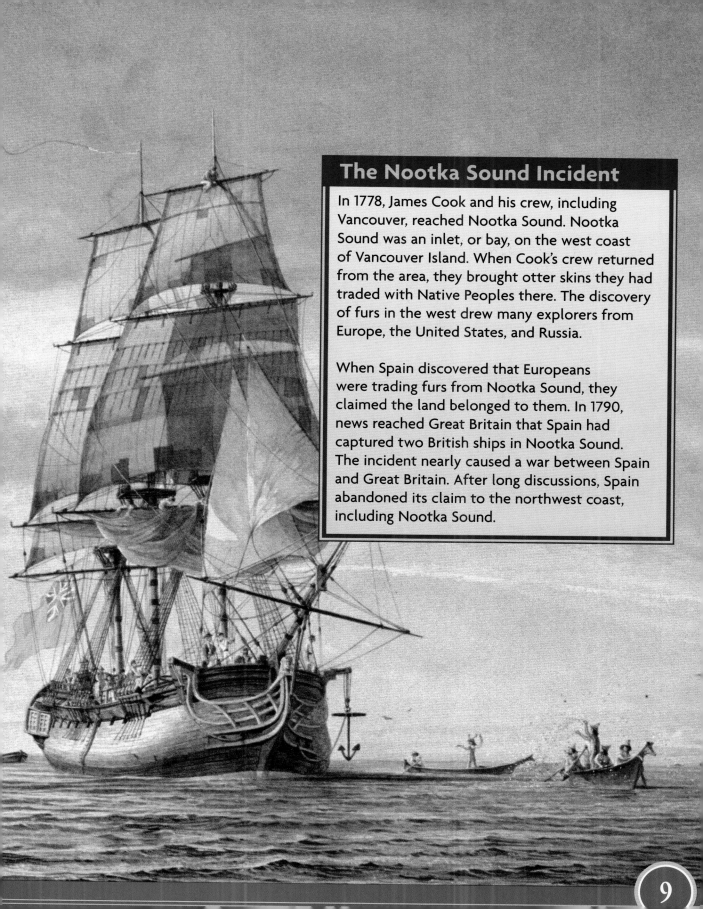

## The Nootka Sound Incident

In 1778, James Cook and his crew, including Vancouver, reached Nootka Sound. Nootka Sound was an inlet, or bay, on the west coast of Vancouver Island. When Cook's crew returned from the area, they brought otter skins they had traded with Native Peoples there. The discovery of furs in the west drew many explorers from Europe, the United States, and Russia.

When Spain discovered that Europeans were trading furs from Nootka Sound, they claimed the land belonged to them. In 1790, news reached Great Britain that Spain had captured two British ships in Nootka Sound. The incident nearly caused a war between Spain and Great Britain. After long discussions, Spain abandoned its claim to the northwest coast, including Nootka Sound.

# Exploring for Riches

In the 1600s and 1700s, Europeans were drawn to North America's natural resources and land. Money, supplies, and the cost of a crew and ship were very expensive. Many explorers asked for funding from independent investors, **merchants**, or the leaders of the countries where they lived.

## Explorer Essentials

Explorers travelled to distant lands hoping they would become wealthy. At the time Vancouver left on his expedition, the British government said it would give $230,000 to the person who discovered the Northwest Passage.

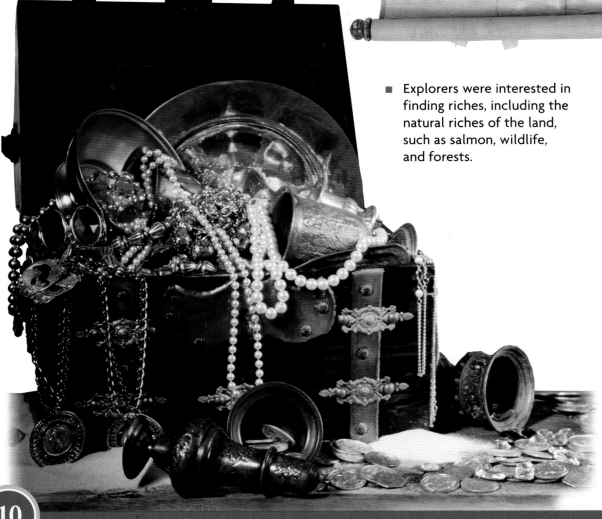

■ Explorers were interested in finding riches, including the natural riches of the land, such as salmon, wildlife, and forests.

Vancouver was a respected seaman and member of the Royal Navy when he was asked to captain his first ship to the Pacific Ocean. The British government paid for his supplies. Vancouver required 2 ships, 145 crewmembers, food, water, weapons, and tools.

- Soon after George Vancouver explored North America's west coast, the Hudson's Bay Company established trading posts in the area.

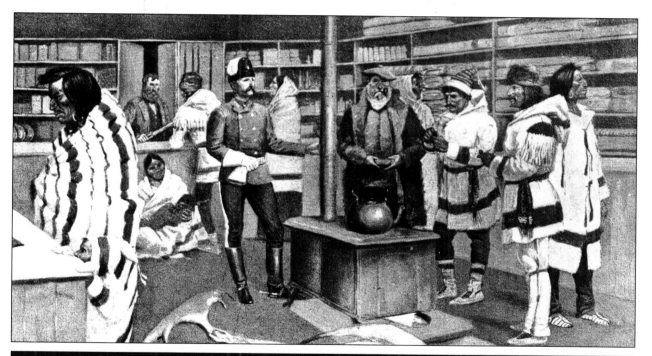

## Passageway from the Pacific

Canada's western coast was a new area of exploration for Europeans. Many explorers, such as Sebastian Cabot, Jacques Cartier, Henry Hudson, and William Baffin, looked for a crossing between the Atlantic and Pacific Oceans. None of them discovered a Northwest Passage. They found waterways leading to Canada's interior instead. By the time Vancouver reached Canada's northwest coast, explorers and traders had settled throughout eastern Canada. The fur trade was established on the east coast. As well, Russian traders managed the fur trade in Alaska. Vancouver's exploration of British Columbia's coast opened the way for other explorers. For example, Sir Alexander Mackenzie followed Vancouver. Mackenzie helped settle British Columbia by exploring the land and setting up trading posts in the province.

# Ships and Tools

George Vancouver only captained one expedition. He spent 4.5 years exploring the coast between California and Alaska. It was the longest expedition in the 1700s. To ensure a successful voyage, Vancouver needed enough food, supplies, tools, and people.

In the 1600s and 1700s, explorers commonly sailed with fleets, or groups of ships. Large fleets allowed captains to carry a greater number of crewmembers and supplies. The ships also offered protection if they encountered enemies. Large fleets helped captains transport goods and resources they traded or discovered during their journeys. Vancouver left Great Britain with two ships, the *Discovery* and the *Chatham*. The *Discovery* was a "sloop," or a type of warship. The *Chatham* was a "tender." It was a smaller ship used to carry supplies and crewmembers. The *Chatham* carried supplies and people that helped repair the *Discovery* when needed.

Captains depended on their crews to help them sail the ship and complete daily chores. Vancouver's crew helped him work the sails and **rigging**, make repairs, and keep the ship in good working order. Most crews in the 1700s included a first mate, cook, carpenter, blacksmith, **boatswain**, **cooper**, and surgeon. Vancouver's crew also included naval officers and sailors, **cartographers**, and a **botanist**.

■ Vancouver's survey on the *Discovery* took longer than expected because he carefully recorded all the details of the land and the coast.

Vancouver used many tools to navigate. These tools included a compass, a **sextant**, and a telescope. Compasses helped sailors determine which direction they were going. Sextants used mirrors to measure the angles between objects, which helped sailors navigate. To map Central and North America's western coasts, Vancouver used measuring chains. Crewmembers rowed the chains from the ship to shore to determine distance. Vancouver also used theolodites. These instruments were used to determine the height of landforms, such as mountains, along the coasts.

■ Cape Mudge is on the west coast of Canada. It was named after Zachary Mudge, who was George Vancouver's first lieutenant on the *Discovery*.

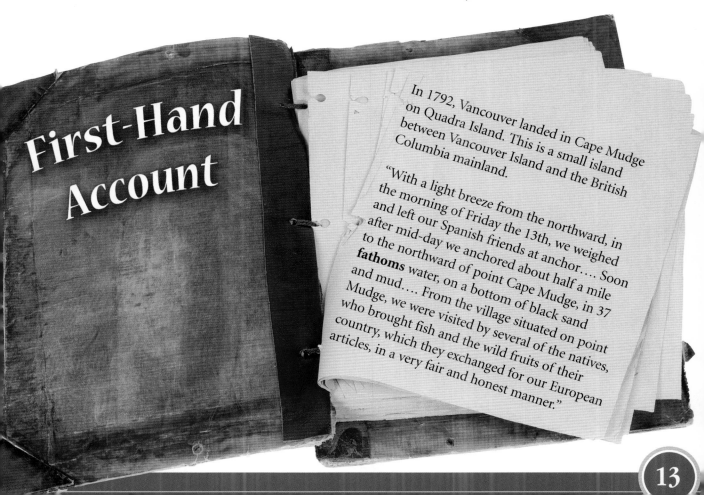

# First-Hand Account

In 1792, Vancouver landed in Cape Mudge on Quadra Island. This is a small island between Vancouver Island and the British Columbia mainland.

"With a light breeze from the northward, in the morning of Friday the 13th, we weighed and left our Spanish friends at anchor…. Soon after mid-day we anchored about half a mile to the northward of point Cape Mudge, in 37 **fathoms** water, on a bottom of black sand and mud…. From the village situated on point Mudge, we were visited by several of the natives, who brought fish and the wild fruits of their country, which they exchanged for our European articles, in a very fair and honest manner."

# Sailing Supplies

It took Vancouver and his crew nearly a year to voyage south from Great Britain to New Zealand. Life at sea was dangerous. The crew was at sea for long periods of time. All food and water had to be stored on board the ship. There was poor **ventilation**, and water leaked into the storerooms. Food often spoiled.

Most ships in the 1600s and 1700s were stocked with hardtack. This was a type of hard biscuit. Hardtack was cooked twice to preserve it in wet conditions. Meals consisted of salted pork, beef, fish, peas, wheat oatmeal, cheese, butter, sugar, oil, vinegar, raisins, and suet, or beef and sheep fat. These foods were very low in vitamin C. Crewmembers often became ill with **scurvy**.

- James Lind was a Scottish doctor who recommended that citrus fruit be included in the diets of British Navy crewmembers so they would not get scurvy.

To prevent scurvy, Vancouver used a diet he learned on board James Cook's voyages. Cook insisted his crew eat foods, such as salad greens, grown on the ship. He also provided lemon and orange **extract**, mustard, **sauerkraut**, and marmalade made from carrots. Many crewmembers complained because they did not like these foods. Still, they were high in vitamin C and prevented Vancouver's crew from getting scurvy.

■ Vancouver's tea was made by soaking spruce needles in water. The spruce tips could be gathered all year, including winter months.

## First-Hand Account

To survive a 4.5-year expedition, Vancouver's ships needed to make frequent stops. They picked up fresh water, fruits, vegetables, and other supplies. Often, they relied on Native Peoples who lived in the regions.

"On landing, which they did without the least hesitation, their behaviour was courteous and friendly in the highest degree. A middle-aged man, to all appearance the chief or principal person of the party, was foremost in shewing marks of the greatest hospitality; and perceiving our party were at breakfast, presented them with water, roasted roots, dried fish, and other articles of food. This person, in return, received some presents, and others were distributed amongst the ladies and some of the party."

# Sailing the Pacific

On April 1, 1791, Vancouver and his crew set sail from Great Britain for the Pacific Ocean. It took 7 months to arrive in Australia. From there, they travelled to New Zealand, Tahiti, and finally to Hawai'i. In Hawai'i, Vancouver and his crew stocked supplies for the long journey north. Vancouver reached the western coast of California in April 1792. The ships travelled along the coast to Nootka Sound.

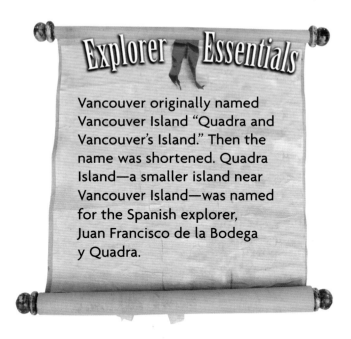

## Explorer Essentials

Vancouver originally named Vancouver Island "Quadra and Vancouver's Island." Then the name was shortened. Quadra Island—a smaller island near Vancouver Island—was named for the Spanish explorer, Juan Francisco de la Bodega y Quadra.

■ The Nootka Native Peoples made totem poles. Some of them are now found in Vancouver and Nootka Sound, British Columbia.

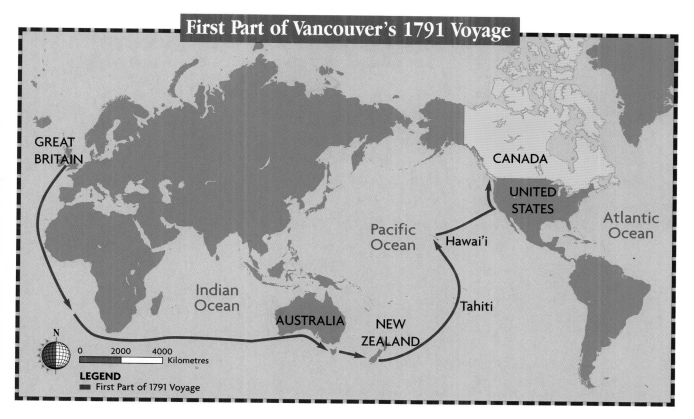

## First Part of Vancouver's 1791 Voyage

GREAT BRITAIN

CANADA

UNITED STATES

Atlantic Ocean

Pacific Ocean

Hawai'i

Indian Ocean

Tahiti

AUSTRALIA

NEW ZEALAND

N

0   2000   4000
Kilometres

LEGEND
First Part of 1791 Voyage

On their way, Vancouver and his crew recorded and mapped the uneven coast. There were many small inlets, rivers, and passages along the coast. The large ships could not get close enough to explore them. Vancouver anchored the larger ships in safe harbours. He sent smaller boats, called cutters, ashore to explore and map the land. In the first year of his voyage, Vancouver located and named several important landmarks. These landmarks included Puget Sound, in present-day Washington in the United States, and Burrard Inlet, the site of present-day Vancouver, British Columbia. George Vancouver also surveyed Vancouver Island. He proved that it was not part of mainland British Columbia.

In August, George Vancouver went to Nootka Sound. He wanted to meet the Spanish representative, Juan Francisco de la Bodega y Quadra. Vancouver and his crew were welcomed. The two men became good friends. Still, they were unable to resolve all the differences between Great Britain and Spain.

# Extended Exploration

In 1793, Vancouver and his crew sailed south to Hawai'i. Winters in the northern Pacific Ocean were very dangerous because of storms, ice, and glaciers, or slow-moving masses of ice. Hawai'i was a good place to rest and repair any damage to the ships.

Vancouver and his crew spent the winter mapping and exploring several Hawai'ian Islands. One of the islands he explored was Oahu, including the areas now known as Waikiki and nearby Pearl Harbor.

- The warm climate of Hawai'i allowed Vancouver and his crew to build up their strength during the winter.

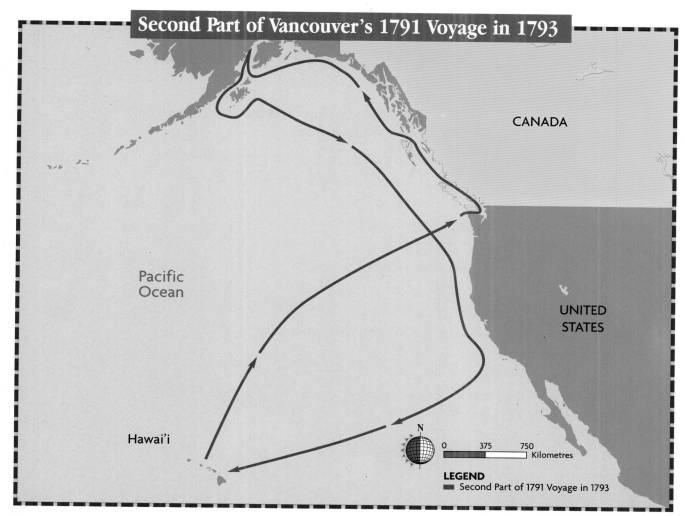

CANADA

Pacific
Ocean

UNITED
STATES

Hawai'i

N

0    375    750
Kilometres

**LEGEND**
■ Second Part of 1791 Voyage in 1793

In May 1793, Vancouver and his crew returned to what is now known as Canada. They spent several months mapping the areas surrounding Vancouver Island and the coast of British Columbia. Vancouver's crew sailed north from Burke Channel. They explored Observatory Inlet, Portland Canal, and Revillagigedo Island in Alaska. In October, Vancouver sailed south again to California and Hawai'i.

## Explorer Essentials

Burrard Inlet is the site where the city of Vancouver, British Columbia, now stands. It was named after Sir Henry Burrard, who sailed with Vancouver in the Royal Navy. The first **settlement**, called Granville, was destroyed in an 1886 fire. When the city was rebuilt, it was named Vancouver, after the explorer.

# The Final Survey

**V**ancouver spent one more season exploring North America's northwest coast. In February 1794, he and his crew travelled through the Hawai'ian Islands for the last time. Vancouver decided to explore the northwest coast from north to south to avoid poor winter weather. On his final trip to the Far North, Vancouver also hoped to finally find the Northwest Passage.

Vancouver and his crew sailed from Cook Inlet to the tip of Baranof Island in Alaska. He named their final Alaska landing spot Port Conclusion, to mark the end of the long journey. Vancouver mapped the entire western coast from California to Alaska. He proved that there was no entrance to the Northwest Passage from the west.

- Vancouver dedicated a total of three summers to the coastal exploration. This exploration ended in August 1794, at Baranof Island.

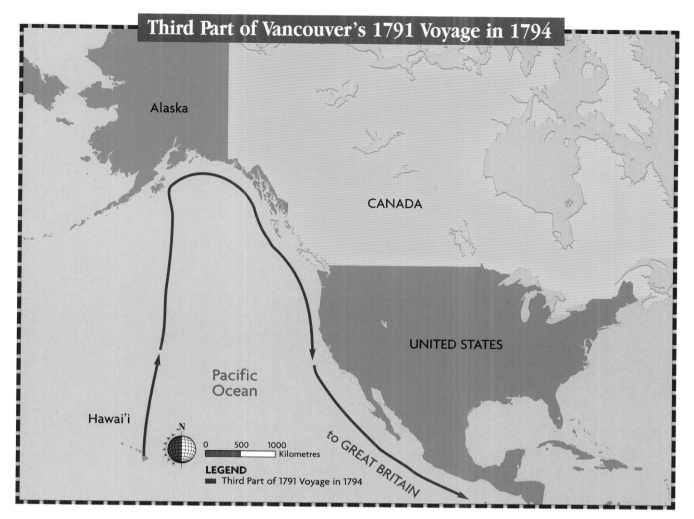

Alaska

CANADA

UNITED STATES

Pacific
Ocean

Hawai'i

N

0  500  1000
Kilometres

to GREAT BRITAIN

**LEGEND**
■ Third Part of 1791 Voyage in 1794

Vancouver and his crew made one final stop at
Nootka Sound before returning to Great Britain.
The Nootka Sound matter with the Spanish still
had not been resolved. Spain and Great Britain
could not agree how much money Great Britain
was to be paid for the two British ships Spain had
captured. Vancouver and his crew were eager to
return home. Still, they waited until Great Britain
said they would send another representative to
Nootka Sound.

The long journey home began in November 1794.
Vancouver's ships sailed south. They stopped in
California, Cocos Island, and Chile before arriving
in London in September 1795.

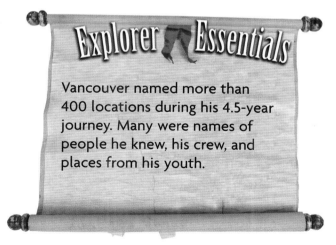

## Explorer Essentials

Vancouver named more than
400 locations during his 4.5-year
journey. Many were names of
people he knew, his crew, and
places from his youth.

# Suffering at Sea and on Land

Life at sea was difficult for Vancouver and his crew. Most explorers voyaged for 1 or 2 years at a time. They returned home, stocked goods, repaired their ships, and prepared for other journeys between expeditions.

Native Peoples helped make Vancouver's journeys successful. In Nootka Sound and Hawai'i, they helped the crew find food and water. However, not all of the Native Peoples were friendly. Sometimes there was conflict between Native Peoples and Europeans. During Vancouver's expedition, some crewmembers were injured.

Vancouver avoided many of the common dangers of long voyages. By returning to Hawai'i during winter, Vancouver missed the poor weather, sheets of floating ice, and icebergs that made the north Pacific difficult to sail. He also fed his crew foods rich in vitamin C so they would not develop scurvy.

Vancouver's crew faced other hardships. On the trip home to Great Britain, the *Chatham* caught fire. The crew managed to put the fire out and prevent the ship from sinking.

■ One of the dangers facing Vancouver's ships was getting caught on rocks. This happened in 1791 with the *Discovery* at Queen Charlotte Strait.

Some crewmembers became sick from eating foods they were not familiar with. Some crewmembers developed a disease called **dysentery**.

Despite these troubles, Vancouver returned to Great Britain with most of his original crew. Only six people died during the entire 4.5-year voyage.

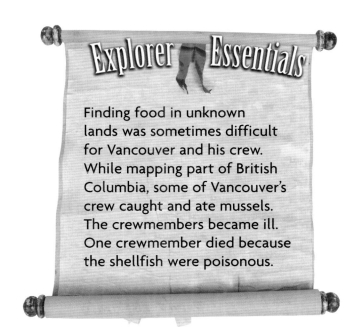

## Explorer Essentials

Finding food in unknown lands was sometimes difficult for Vancouver and his crew. While mapping part of British Columbia, some of Vancouver's crew caught and ate mussels. The crewmembers became ill. One crewmember died because the shellfish were poisonous.

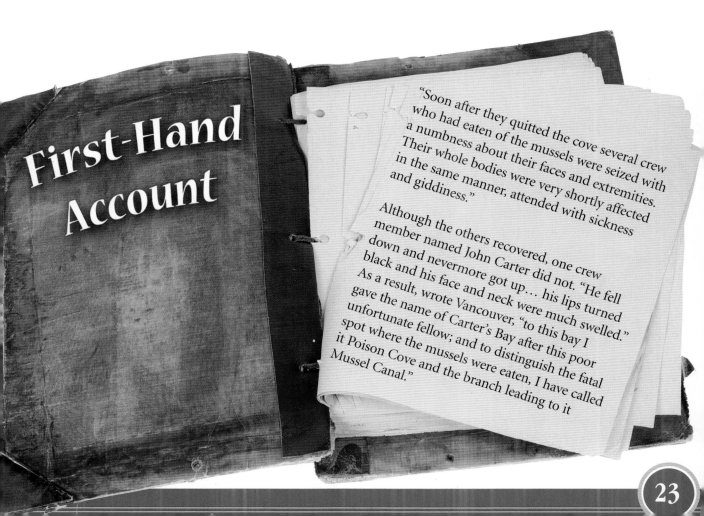

## First-Hand Account

"Soon after they quitted the cove several crew who had eaten of the mussels were seized with a numbness about their faces and extremities. Their whole bodies were very shortly affected in the same manner, attended with sickness and giddiness."

Although the others recovered, one crew member named John Carter did not. "He fell down and nevermore got up... his lips turned black and his face and neck were much swelled." As a result, wrote Vancouver, "to this bay I gave the name of Carter's Bay after this poor unfortunate fellow; and to distinguish the fatal spot where the mussels were eaten, I have called it Poison Cove and the branch leading to it Mussel Canal."

# Lasting Achievements and Legacies

During Vancouver's lifetime, he had many successes. He determined that there was no entrance to the Northwest Passage along the coast he explored. The maps created on Vancouver's voyage were the first detailed maps of the western coast of North America. Future explorers depended on Vancouver's maps. The maps were used for exploration and settlement of the west coast of Canada and the United States.

Vancouver's maps were included in his book *A Voyage of Discovery to the North Pacific Ocean, and Round the World*. The book described his journey to the western coast of North America. Vancouver died in 1798 before the book was finished. His brother, John, finished it on Vancouver's behalf. It was the first book that detailed a British explorer's adventures.

Vancouver's legacy lives on in the many landmarks he named throughout Canada. There are also places named after him. In addition to Vancouver, British Columbia, a city named Vancouver is located in the state of Washington in the United States.

Some cities in British Columbia, the United States, and Great Britain have statues and plaques of Vancouver. In Canada, the city hall in Vancouver has a statue of Captain George Vancouver. A plaque on the statue describes Vancouver's 1792 visit. Vanier Park, in the Kitsilano area of Vancouver, also has a statue of Vancouver.

■ In the early 1800s, an unknown artist painted a portrait of Vancouver.

A plaque in North Vancouver recognizes Vancouver for naming Burrard Inlet. There is a bust of Vancouver on the Burrard Street bridge in Vancouver. At the legislature buildings in Victoria, the capital of British Columbia, the roof-top dome has a gilded, or gold, statue of Vancouver keeping watch over the harbour.

In Vancouver, Washington, there is a Captain George Vancouver Monument at the Columbia River waterfront. At a museum in Honolulu, Hawai'i, there is a portrait of Vancouver with a plaque that reads: "George Vancouver: English navigator and a true friend to Hawai'ians." A totem pole, located in Kihei, Maui, Hawai'i, was made as a monument to Vancouver.

The birthplace of Vancouver in King's Lynn, Norfolk, Great Britain, has a statue of him. It was created to commemorate the 200th anniversary of his death. The City of Vancouver, in British Columbia, donated money toward this project.

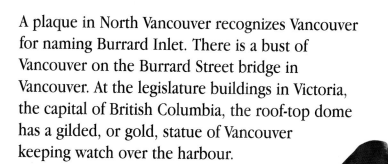

## Explorer Essentials

Vancouver built a good relationship with the people of Hawai'i. He encouraged the people of Hawai'i to join Great Britain. Wars with France at the time prevented Great Britain from claiming the island. In 1898, Hawai'i joined the United States.

■ A bronze statue of Vancouver was erected in 2000 in King's Lynn, Great Britain.

# Explorer Expeditions

Many explorers voyaged to Canada in search of riches and new lands to claim for European merchants.

BRITISH COLUMBIA

Rocky Mountain
Portage House

Peace River

CANADA

Pacific
Ocean

Fort
George

Fraser
River

Vancouver
Island

Hope

## Simon Fraser

Simon Fraser was of **Loyalist** origin through his father. He became a partner with the North West Company. Fraser explored the area west of the Rocky Mountains.

← Fraser 1805
← Fraser 1808

## George Vancouver

George Vancouver was a skilled navigator and mapmaker for Great Britain. He tried to find the Northwest Passage, but was unsuccessful. Vancouver explored the Hawai'ian Islands, the west coast of Canada, and Alaska.

← Vancouver 1793
← Vancouver 1794

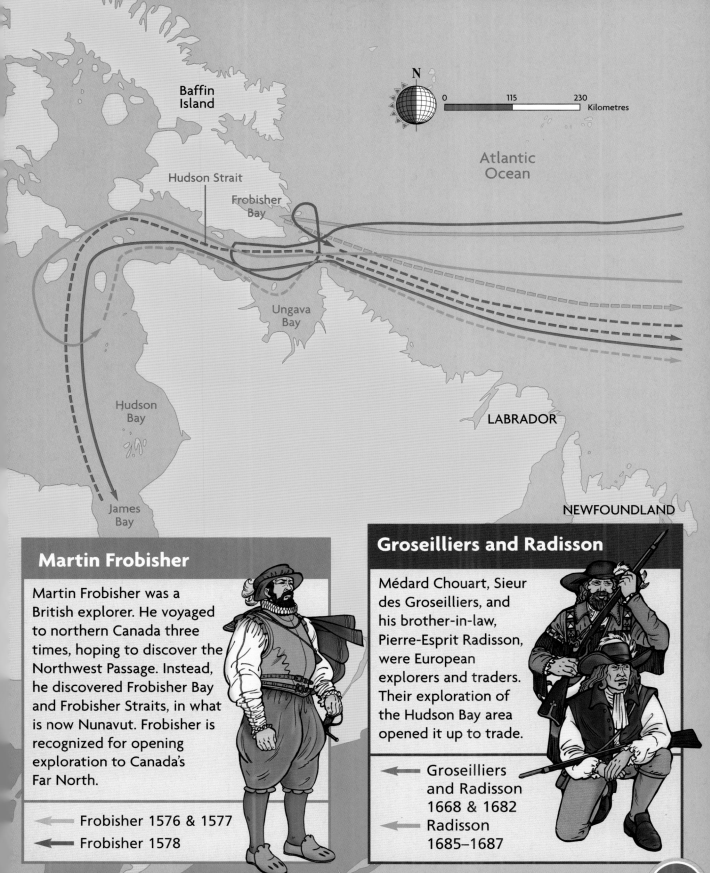

Baffin
Island

Hudson Strait

Frobisher
Bay

Atlantic
Ocean

0    115    230
Kilometres

Ungava
Bay

Hudson
Bay

LABRADOR

James
Bay

NEWFOUNDLAND

## Martin Frobisher

Martin Frobisher was a British explorer. He voyaged to northern Canada three times, hoping to discover the Northwest Passage. Instead, he discovered Frobisher Bay and Frobisher Straits, in what is now Nunavut. Frobisher is recognized for opening exploration to Canada's Far North.

← Frobisher 1576 & 1577
← Frobisher 1578

## Groseilliers and Radisson

Médard Chouart, Sieur des Groseilliers, and his brother-in-law, Pierre-Esprit Radisson, were European explorers and traders. Their exploration of the Hudson Bay area opened it up to trade.

← Groseilliers and Radisson 1668 & 1682
← Radisson 1685–1687

# Time Line

**1757** Vancouver is born in King's Lynn, Great Britain.

**1771** Vancouver joins Great Britain's Royal Navy.

**1772** Vancouver accompanies James Cook on Cook's second voyage in the Pacific Ocean.

**1776** Vancouver accompanies James Cook on Cook's third voyage in the Pacific Ocean.

**1780** Vancouver is made a lieutenant in the Royal Navy.

**1780–1789** Vancouver serves in the Caribbean Sea as part of the Royal Navy.

**1791** Vancouver captains an expedition to the northwest coast of North America.

**1792** Vancouver explores the west coast of North America. He discovers Burrard Inlet and proves that Vancouver Island is not part of the mainland.

**1793** Vancouver maps the areas and islands surrounding Vancouver Island and part of the British Columbia mainland.

**1794** Vancouver explores the coast of Alaska and its surrounding islands.

**1795** Vancouver returns to Great Britain and **retires** from the Royal Navy.

**1796** Vancouver begins writing his book, *A Voyage of Discovery to the North Pacific Ocean, and Round the World.*

**1798** Vancouver dies in Petersham, Great Britain.

■ An aerial view of the city of Vancouver, British Columbia, shows some of the areas Vancouver named, including Burrard Inlet.

# Make a Map

Vancouver made the first detailed map of the northwest coast of North America. With the help of a friend, you can make a map of an area in your own home.

### Materials
grid paper
markers, pens, or pencils
string

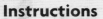

### Instructions
1. Pick an area to map. Good places to start are a room in your house or your yard. Ask a friend to help you make a map.
2. Take one end of some string. Hold it against a wall on the edge of your room or yard. Have a friend walk to the other end of the area you are mapping with the other end of the string. Lay the string down on the ground.
3. Measure the string by taking steps along its length. Record the number of steps lengthwise. Then, repeat these steps while measuring the width of the room or yard. Record the number of steps widthwise.
4. After determining the length and width of the room or yard, draw the area on the piece of paper. Each step is one square on the grid paper. This is the outline of your room or yard.
5. Using the string, measure the distances between objects in the area being mapped. Start with something along the edge of the room or yard. Measure how far it is from other objects.
6. Once you have mapped everything in your area, label the objects you included on the map.

# Quiz

1. How long was Vancouver's only expedition?

2. How old was Vancouver when he first sailed on a ship? What was the name of the captain he sailed with?

3. In what year did Vancouver prove that Vancouver Island was not part of the mainland?

4. Why was Vancouver sent on his expedition?

5. Outside of Canada, what group of Native Peoples became good friends with Vancouver and helped him?

6. What did Vancouver feed his crew to prevent scurvy?

7. What did Vancouver do when he returned to Great Britain?

8. Who helped Vancouver finish writing his book?

9. What name did Vancouver give the area where the present-day city of Vancouver, British Columbia, stands?

10. What were some of the tools Vancouver used to navigate and make maps?

## Answers

1. 4.5 years, from 1791 to 1795
2. 13 years old; James Cook
3. 1792
4. to map the Pacific coast of North America; to determine if there was an entrance to the Northwest Passage on the coast; and to help resolve the Nootka Sound incident
5. the people of Hawai'i
6. salad greens, lemon and orange extract, mustard, sauerkraut, and marmalade made from carrots
7. He retired from the navy and began to write a book.
8. his brother, John
9. Burrard Inlet
10. compasses, sextants, telescopes, measuring chains, and theodolites

# Web Sites

To learn about Vancouver, visit:
Historica: The Canadian Encyclopedia. Under search, type Captain George Vancouver.
www.thecanadianencyclopedia.com

For information about Vancouver and other explorers, visit:
Library and Archives Canada: Pathfinders & Passageways
www.collectionscanada.ca/explorers/h24-1730-e.html

To learn about Vancouver and the city of Vancouver, visit:
Discover Vancouver. Scroll down and click on Captain George Vancouver.
www.discovervancouver.com/GVB

# Books

Armitage, Doreen. *Burrard Inlet*. Madeira Park, BC: Harbour Publishing, 2001.

Fisher, Robin and Hugh Johnston, eds. *From Maps to Metaphors: The Pacific World of George Vancouver*. Vancouver, BC: UBC Press, 1993.

McKinney, Sam. *Sailing with Vancouver: A Modern Sea Dog, Antique Charts and a Voyage Through Time*. Victoria, BC: TouchWood Editions, 2004.

# Glossary

**boatswain** the crewmember in charge of equipment and other crewmembers' duties

**botanist** a person who studies plants

**bowsprit** the pointed piece of metal or wood that extends from the front of a ship

**cartographers** people who makes maps or charts

**continent** a large expanse of land

**cooper** a person who makes and repairs barrels

**dysentery** a disease of the intestine

**extract** a concentrated solution

**fathoms** measurement equal to 1.83 metres

**lieutenant** a high-ranking member of the military

**Loyalist** person who supported Great Britain during the American Revolution

**merchants** people who buy and sell goods

**navigator** the person who plans which direction a ship will travel

**Northwest Passage** a water route from the Atlantic Ocean to the Pacific Ocean through the Arctic archipelago of northern Canada and along the northern coast of Alaska

**ports** harbours where ships load and unload goods

**retires** stops working for a living

**rigging** the ropes and chains on a ship that support and work the sails

**sauerkraut** sour cabbage

**scurvy** a disease caused by a lack of vitamin C that causes infected gums, loose teeth, and sores on the skin

**settlement** a community

**sextant** a tool used in navigation to measure latitude and longitude

**surveyed** measured an area of land in order to determine its form, size, and position

**ventilation** allow fresh air to flow and replace stale air

# Index